KEYS TO
Contentment

A STUDY OF PHILIPPIANS

SHARON A. STEELE

Gospel Light

AGLOW.
INTERNATIONAL

Gospel Light is an evangelical Christian publisher dedicated to serving the local church. We believe God's vision for Gospel Light is to provide church leaders with biblical, user-friendly materials that will help them evangelize, disciple and minister to children, youth and families.

We hope this Gospel Light resource will help you discover biblical truth for your own life and help you minister to adults. God bless you in your work.

For a free catalog of resources from Gospel Light please contact your Christian supplier or call 1-800-4-GOSPEL.

PUBLISHING STAFF
William T. Greig, Publisher
Dr. Elmer L. Towns, Senior Consulting Publisher
Dr. Gary S. Greig, Senior Consulting Editor
Jill Honodel, Editor
Pam Weston, Assistant Editor
Kyle Duncan, Associate Publisher
Bayard Taylor, M.Div., Editor, Theological and Biblical Issues
Debi Thayer, Designer
Eva Gibson, Contributing Writer

Aglow International is an interdenominational organization of Christian women. Our mission is to lead women to Jesus Christ and provide opportunity for Christian women to grow in their faith and minister to others.

Our publications are used to help women find a personal relationship with Jesus Christ, to enhance growth in their Christian experience, and to help them recognize their roles and relationships according to Scripture.

For more information about our organization, please write to Aglow International, P.O. Box 1749, Edmonds, WA 98020-1749, U.S.A., or call (425) 775-7282. For ordering or information about the Aglow studies call (800) 793-8126.

CONTENTS

FOREWORD

When the apostle Paul poured out his heart in letters to the young churches in Asia, he was responding to his apostolic call to shepherd those tender flocks. They needed encouragement in their new life in Jesus. They needed solid doctrine. They needed truth from someone who had an intimate relationship with God and with them.

Did Paul know as he was writing that these simple letters would form the bulk of the New Testament? We can be confident that the Holy Spirit did! How like God to use Paul's relationship with these churches to cement His plan and purpose in their lives, and, generations later, in ours.

We in Aglow can relate to Paul's desire to bond those young churches together in the faith. After 1967, when Aglow fellowships began bubbling up across the United States and in other countries, they needed encouragement. They needed to know the fullness of who they were in Christ. They needed relationship. Like Paul, our desire to reach out and nurture from far away birthed a series of Bible studies that have fed thousands since 1973 when our first study, *Genesis*, was published. Our studies share heart-to-heart, giving Christians new insights about themselves and their relationships with and in God.

God's generous Spirit has recently provided us a rewarding new relationship with Gospel Light Publications. Together we are publishing our Aglow classics, as well as a selection of exciting new studies. Gospel Light began as a publishing ministry much in the same way Aglow began publishing Bible studies. Henrietta Mears, one of its visionary founders, formed Gospel Light in response to requests from churches across America for the Sunday School materials she had written for the First Presbyterian Church in Hollywood, California. Gospel Light remains a strong ministry-minded witness for the gospel around the world.

Our heart's desire is that these studies will continue to kindle the minds of women and men, touch their hearts, and refresh spirits with the light and life a loving Savior abundantly supplies.

This study, *Keys to Contentment* by Sharon Steele, contains God's wisdom for maintaining a satisfied heart, whatever your circumstance. I know its contents will reward you richly.

— Jane Hansen
International President, Aglow International

INTRODUCTION

Jesus said, "I came that they might have life, and might have it abundantly" (John 10:10). Yet people today in all walks of life are dissatisfied, living in anguish with little or no peace of mind, no contentment. Even many Christians are strangers to the rich, full, satisfying life that Jesus said we could have. Although they desire a life of peace and contentment, they haven't yet found the way to achieve it.

Paul, the author of the Epistle to the Philippians, wrote, "I have learned to be content in whatever circumstances I am" (Philippians 4:11). As he wrote these words, the apostle was in prison for the cause of the gospel, facing an uncertain future. He realized his life could be snuffed out at any moment. At other times he'd been hungry, in need, in desperate circumstances, but he had learned to be content. What was the secret of his contentment in every situation?

As we study Philippians, we will see characteristics in Paul's life and principles in his teachings that led to this full, rich, contented life for him.

I would encourage you to put these principles into practice in your life and see what God will do. Malachi 3:10 encourages us to test God in our giving and see Him "open for you the windows of heaven, and pour out for you a blessing until it overflows." I believe we can also test God with the principles we learn in this study. As we learn and apply them, we can expect God to pour out His blessing on us, meeting our every need. We will find contentment in Christ. We will experience the abundant life that Jesus came to give.

AN OVERVIEW OF THE STUDY

This Bible study is divided into four sections:

- A CLOSER LOOK AT THE PROBLEM defines the problem and the goal of the study.

- A CLOSER LOOK AT GOD'S TRUTH gets you into God's Word. What does God have to say about the problem? How can you begin to apply God's Word as you work through each lesson?

- A CLOSER LOOK AT MY OWN HEART will help you clarify and further apply truth. It will also give guidance as you work towards change.

- ACTION STEPS I CAN TAKE TODAY is designed to help you concentrate on immediate steps of action.

YOU WILL NEED

- A Bible.

- A notebook—Some questions may require more space than is given in this study book. You may also want to journal additional thoughts or feelings that come up as you go through the lessons.

- Time to meditate on what you're learning. You will be working through a lot of Scripture in these lessons. Giving the Holy Spirit time to personalize His Words to your heart will help you experience the abundance of contentment and joy that can only come from Him.

HOW TO START AND LEAD A SMALL GROUP

<hr/>

One key to starting and leading a small group is to ask yourself, What would Jesus do and how would he do it? Jesus began His earthly ministry with a small group of disciples. The fact of His presence made wherever He was a safe place to be. Think of a small group as a safe place. It is a place that reflects God's heart, God's hands. The way in which Jesus lived and worked with His disciples is a basic small group model that we are able to draw both from direction and nurture.

Paul exhorts us to "walk in love, as Christ also has loved us and given Himself for us" (Ephesians 5:2, *NKJV*). We, as His earthly reflections, are privileged to walk in His footsteps, to help bind up the brokenhearted as He did or simply to listen with a compassionate heart. Whether you use this book as a Bible study, or as a focus point for a support group, a church or home group, walking in love means that we "bear one another's burdens" (Galatians 6:2, *NKJV*). The loving atmosphere provided by a small group can nourish, sustain and lift us up as nothing else does.

Jesus walked in love and spoke from an honest heart. In His endless well of compassion He never misplaced truth. Rather, he surrounded it with mercy. Those who left His presence felt good about themselves because Jesus used truth to point them in the right direction for their lives. When He spoke about the sinful woman who washed Jesus' feet with her tears and wiped them with her hair, He did not deny her sin. He said, "her sins, which are many, are forgiven, for she loved much" (Luke 7:47, *NKJV*). That's honesty without condemnation.

Jesus was a model of servant leadership. "Whoever desires to become great among you shall be your servant. And whoever of you desires to be first shall be slave of all" (Mark 10:43,47, *NKJV*). One of the key skills a group leader possesses is to be an encourager of the group's members to grow spiritually. Keeping in personal contact with each member of the group, especially if one is absent, tells each one that he/she is important to the group. Other skills an effective group leader will develop are: being a good listener, guiding the discussion, and guiding the group to deal with any conflicts that arise within it.

Whether you're a veteran or brand new to small group leadership, virtually every group you lead will be different in personality and dynamics. The constant is the presence of Jesus Christ, and when He is at the group's center, everything else can come together.

YOU'RE INVITED!

To grow...

> *To develop and reach maturity; thrive; to spring up; come into existence from a source;*

with a group

> *An assemblage of persons gathered or located together; a number of individuals considered together because of similarities;*

To explore...

> *To investigate systematically; examine; search into or range over for the purpose of discovery;*

new topics

> *Subjects of discussion or conversation.*

Meeting on

Date _____ Time_____

Located at

Place _____

_____

Contact _____

Phone_____

One

TRUST IN JESUS

There is no other epistle that sings more joyfully than Paul's letter to the Philippians. Yet Paul wrote it near the end of his life when he was in prison.

His letter shouts with joy triumphant: "Come, share my joy as you have shared my conflict," he invites. The fact that Jesus Christ loved him and gave Himself for him is the high note of his letter.

What was Paul's secret? How was he able to trust Jesus when everything seemed to be going against him? How had he found contentment in such a negative situation? This chapter will turn our minds and hearts in God's direction. As we do, we will see Paul's complete trust in Jesus. It is only as we experience this kind of trust that we will find the secret of true contentment.

A Closer Look at the Problem

LIFE IS HARD

Even though we may not be in prison, we all face difficult situations. We live in a sinful world and life is often hard. Not only that, other people seem to have it a whole lot easier than we do. How can we trust that God is really for us? How can we find true contentment and joy?

This study will help you discover how trust in Jesus will free you for joy. Let's begin the study of Philippians with a look at the story of the church's beginning.

A Closer Look at God's Truth

The book of Philippians was a letter to the believers at Philippi, written by Paul from his prison cell, most likely in Rome. Paul had been instrumental in founding the Philippian church during his second missionary journey. The beginning of this church is the exciting story of how God can lead and use a willing servant.

1. Read Acts 16:6-10. Why didn't Paul and his companions preach in Asia or Bithynia?

   Spirit prevented them

   What happened to Paul at Troas?

   vision — Macedonia needs him

   What did Paul decide to do and why (v. 10)?

   go

   How long did it take Paul to make his decision?

   at once

Paul had an intimate relationship with God. He not only heard what the Holy Spirit said, but upon receiving direction, he acted immediately and in complete faith.

What are some of the ways the Holy Spirit directs people today?

Share a specific instance when you have been led by the Holy Spirit.

2. Read Acts 16:11-15. At what city in Macedonia did they stop?

Philippi

Where did they go on the Sabbath day? Why?

out city gate to river to find place of prayer

Whom did they find there?

Lydia w/ women g athered there.

What was Lydia's response to the message she heard?

Opened her heart & respond

What happened as a result of her response?

household baptized, + Paul & Co. invited to her home.

What a marvelous example of the work of the Holy Spirit! Paul and his company were led to Philippi by the Holy Spirit, and as they shared, the Lord opened the hearts of the women who listened. When Christians respond to the leadership of the Holy Spirit in sharing the message of Jesus, God will open the hearts of those who listen.

3. Read Acts 16:16-24. Where were Paul and his companions going (v. 16)?

to a place of prayer

Who met them on the way?

a slave girl who predicted the future & earned money for her masters

What did she say about Paul and his companions?

that they were servants of God, telling others how to be saved.

How long did she continue saying this?

for many days

What did Paul do as a result?

was troubled & "cured" her

Why do you think Paul cast this demon out?

distracting + not from a "worthy source,"

By what power did Paul cast it out?

in the name of Jesus —

Why did her owners become so angry?

no more money

What happened to Paul and Silas as a result?

Stripped, beaten, prison

Even though Paul and Silas were called to preach in Philippi, Satan attacked. Satan will frequently attack the Christians who are obeying God's call. Sometimes, he attacks with little annoyances; sometimes, with huge problems or temptations.

What are some ways Satan attacks Christians today?

4. Paul had power over Satan because he had the power of Jesus Christ available to him. Read 1 John 4:4. What is promised in this verse?

We are dear children come from God - + the one in us is greater than "one in the world."

What key to overcoming Satan is found in James 4:7?

Be patient!

We too have the power of Jesus available to us. When we fight Satan in Jesus' name and in His power, we can win. When we resist him, he will flee.

Share an experience in which you won a victory over Satan's attack.

5. Read Acts 16:25-34. What were Paul and Silas doing around midnight?

Praying + singing hymns

Who was listening to them?

other prisoners

Why do you think Paul and Silas were able to pray and sing after being beaten and thrown into prison?

Paul and Silas were able to praise the Lord during this difficult time because they totally trusted Jesus. They knew He loved them and would take care of them even though everything looked bleak and they were in pain and discomfort. Their trust in Jesus gave them an attitude of praise and rejoicing.

What miracle of God took place (v. 26)?

Earthquake – doors threw open

How do we know this was a miracle of God and not an ordinary earthquake?

Why did the jailer decide to kill himself?

for loss of prisoners

What question did he ask after he saw all the prisoners were safe?

what must I do to be saved

What do you think led him to ask that question?

How did Paul and Silas answer his question?

Believe in the Lord Jesus

What evidence do we have that the Philippian jailer became a believer?

He was baptized & his family —

According to verse 34, what emotion did the jailer experience as a result of believing?

joy — to whole fame

The most essential ingredient in finding joy or contentment is that we, like the Philippian jailer, believe in the Lord. Until a person accepts Jesus Christ as Savior and Lord, he/she can never experience God's true peace and joy. When the jailer trusted Jesus to save him, he experienced the joy and contentment that only God can give.

6. Read Psalms 4:5-8; 16:7-11; 91:14-16; 107:6-9; 144:15. How does our relationship with God affect our experiencing joy and satisfaction in life?

trust safety — heart filled greater than other source

When God created man, He created him for fellowship with Himself. Although we don't always recognize it, we are created with a natural desire, a longing for God. Until we experience that personal relationship with Him, we cannot know fullness of joy and peace.

7. Read the story of the young man who came to Jesus in Luke 18:18-23. Although this young man was already living a moral life and had riches, he came to Jesus because he had a need—the hunger in his heart was unsatisfied.

Upon seeing him Jesus recognized that this man's riches were the most important thing in his life. They had become his god. When the man refused to follow Jesus, he went away in sorrow.

It's important to realize that he became very sad because he had made the wrong choice. Jesus came to give an abundant life, but He cannot give that abundance and peace unless a person is willing to make Him the Lord of his or her life. Anything we value more than God becomes, in effect, another god in our lives.

What are some of the gods prevalent in our society today?

What are some of the gods in your life?

A Closer Look at My Own Heart

Paul told the Philippian jailer to believe on the Lord Jesus, in other words, to trust in Jesus. The young ruler trusted in his good life and his riches, and they were not enough to make him right with God. Romans 6:23 says that "the wages of sin is death." If we were to sin only one time in our entire life, that would be enough to separate us from God. Because the young man was not sinless, he could not find peace with God through his works.

No one can be made right with God by works, but God has provided a remedy for our sin. He sent Jesus who was without sin to die on the cross and pay the penalty for our sin. He takes our sinfulness upon Himself and gives us His righteousness (see 2 Corinthians 5:21). Our part is to trust Jesus to forgive our sins and receive Him by personal invitation.

8. Read the following Scripture passages and answer the questions.

John 14:6—What is the *only* way you can come to God?

through Him

Revelation 3:20—What does Jesus promise?

He stands at the door & knocks & if anyone hears his voice & opens the door – He'll come in & eat w/him

John 1:12—What do you become when you receive Jesus?

children of God – born of God

Romans 10:9—What is promised in this verse and what do you need to do to receive it?

confess w/your mouth Jesus is Lord & believe in your heart God raised Him from the dead, you will be saved.

Action Steps I Can Take Today

9. If you do not know Jesus as your Savior, you can know Him today. Remember His invitation in Revelation 3:20. If anyone will open the door, "I will come in." If you would like to open the door of your heart to Jesus, pray this prayer:

Dear God, I know I can never have peace with You through my efforts. I am a sinner, and I am truly sorry. I believe Jesus died for me, and I trust that His death paid the penalty for my sins. I open the door of my heart to receive Jesus as my personal Savior and Lord. Thank You, Jesus, for coming into my life, forgiving my sins and saving me.

If you sincerely prayed this prayer, where is Jesus right now (see Revelation 3:20)?

What did you become when you received Christ (see John 1:12,13)?

What does God promise to you when you believe in Jesus (see 1 John 5:12,13)?

He who has the son has life.

10. If you know Jesus as your Savior, how deep is your trust? Think through the story of Paul and Silas in Acts 16:35-40. How does their trust in God compare to yours?

Paul and Silas were in jail just long enough for God to do His good work in the lives of the Philippian jailer and his family. When they were thrown into prison, Paul and Silas did not complain and blame God. Instead, they sang and praised Him.

They were able to sing and praise because they knew God was in control of every area of their lives. He was at work and they trusted Him to do what was best for them. Because they trusted, they could rejoice.

11. Is there a situation in your life in which you need to trust God even though it appears hopeless? Write about it in your journal. Then thank God for it by praising Him for being in control of your life and working in your particular situation even when you may not be able to see it.

12. Paul's words in Ephesians 3:20,21 will increase your faith. Write the verses on a file card and place it where you can see it each day. Each day relate the verse to your situation and ask God to help you trust Him more.

He does immeasurably more than we ask or imagine ~ it is His power at work in us.

- *Two* -

PRAISE AND REJOICE

———∞∞∞———

A pastor tells this story of a couple who talked with him shortly after the unexpected death of their son.

> Early in our ministry a family moved to our town on a Monday. On Wednesday at four o'clock, their four-year-old son climbed up on the davenport and fell asleep. Not too unusual—but when they called him for supper at five o'clock, he didn't respond. The child had died.
>
> They called the doctor and the doctor called me. I met the parents for the first time. Tearful? Yes. Brokenhearted? Of course. But as they talked something happened. They shared about what this son had meant to them and how much joy he had brought into their home. They told stories from his life. Thankful for the years they had had together, they asked God to help them through this difficult time.
>
> As I shared this couple's pain, I couldn't help but think *My own son is the same age as the boy who died. If it had been my son who was taken, would I have had the attitude of trust and thanksgiving that they expressed?*

In this chapter we will learn how Paul's trust in Jesus gave him a grateful spirit toward God and others. Because of this trust, he was able to praise and rejoice in the midst of trouble. We will also see that praising and rejoicing are important steps leading to contentment.

A Closer Look at the Problem

COMMANDED TO PRAISE

God commands that we praise Him and that we thank Him at all times (see Psalm 34:1; 1 Thessalonians 5:18). When we respond in obedience, even though circumstances look hopeless, God can use those bad circumstances to bring glory to Himself and maturity to us. It did just that for the young couple who lost their son, and now whenever this story is told, men and women marvel at the power of God working peace and joy in the face of one of life's greatest losses.

When we praise God, we show that we trust Him even if we don't see His hand at work at the time. Verbalizing our praise for a difficult situation releases the fear and anger inside us and allows God to bring something good out of it (see Romans 8:28).

1. Yet so often, instead of rejoicing and praising God, we grumble and complain. Read Psalm 106:13-15,24-27. What happened to the Israelites when they grumbled instead of rejoiced?

   forgot what He'd done for them - not wait for His counsel so a wasting disease came

God was taking care of the Israelites, but they complained and grumbled. He finally gave them what they asked for, but they suffered physically and they spiritually moved away from God. When we complain about what God allows in our lives, it will affect us physically and we will begin to wither spiritually. By contrast when we rejoice, we will begin to grow stronger in the Spirit and free God to take our difficult situations and turn them into something beautiful.

He did it for the young couple whose small son died. He did it for Paul when he was in prison. He can do the same for you in whatever situation you might be facing.

A Closer Look at God's Truth

2. Read Philippians 1:1. How did Paul describe himself and Timothy?

bondServants of Christ Jesus

The Greek word that is translated bond-servant can also be translated as <u>slave</u>.

What picture comes to your mind as you think of a bond-servant or a slave? To whom does a slave belong? What does a slave do?

— owner   whatever he's told
— in earthly, at mercy of whims of your owner - but they
terms   could trust His goodness

3. Read 1 Peter 1:18,19. According to Peter, with *what* were believers, including Paul, bought?

precious blood of the lamb - not w/ gold or silver,
or perishable items

It's important to recognize that because Paul trusted in Jesus, he willingly gave himself to God. When Jesus died on the cross, He paid the price for Paul's salvation, but Paul also made a choice. He could have chosen to remain a slave to sin with death as the end result. Or he could have chosen, as he did, to belong to Christ, receiving His eternal and abundant life and willingly becoming His slave.

4. Read Philippians 1:3-8. How often did Paul thank God for the Philippians?

all prayers — all the time —
when remembering them —
they're in his heart

What was Paul's prayer filled with?

joy *& love for those he'd put in his heart*

List several reasons why Paul was able to pray for the Philippians with joy and thankfulness.

fellow partakers of grace, shared a bond

5. Read 2 Corinthians 8:1-5. In this chapter, as Paul wrote to the Corinthian church, he told them of the Macedonian churches. Remember that Philippi was the chief city in Macedonia, and you can see from Paul's comments to the Corinthians why he felt such deep love and gratitude toward the Philippians.

How are the physical circumstances of the Macedonian churches described (see v. 2)?

in extreme poverty

What had they done in spite of the trouble they were facing?

give beyond their means

How did they look upon this act of giving (see v. 4)?

a privilege to share the service of giving

they begged for the chance

What did they experience in the midst of their affliction and deep poverty (see v. 2)?

overflowing joy

22

How much had they given (see v. 3)?

- beyond their means.
- a suffering church reached out to help

What had they given first (see v. 5)?

themselves - to the Lord

How did this sacrificial giving relate to their abundance of joy?

great ROI

How did their giving reflect their trust in Jesus?

either no fear of worsened circumstances or

6. Read Romans 15:26,27. What was their attitude in giving as described in these verses?

pleased to do it

Why did they feel indebted to the Jewish Christians?

shared in their blessings -

A great persecution toward Christians had arisen in Jerusalem during this period. That, along with a famine, made life very difficult for the Jerusalem believers. The Philippian Christians were so grateful to the Jews for sharing the gospel of Christ that they wanted to share their material possessions with them. Their deep gratitude and their joy in the Lord resulted in a generous offering beyond their ability to give. In addition to aiding Jerusalem Christians, they gave generously toward supporting Paul in his ministry (see 2 Corinthians 11:9). One of the main purposes in Paul's writing the letter to the Philippians was to express his deep gratitude.

How do you feel toward the person or persons who shared the gospel with you?

wow — thanks so much —

Do you feel you owe her/him/them anything?

to keep going continued growth in the Lord. —

7. Read Philippians 4:10-19. What was Paul's reason for rejoicing (see v. 10)?

they are concerned about him —

Why hadn't they sent help sooner?

didn't have an opportunity? maybe they didn't know... distance

What had Paul learned (see vv. 11-13)?

to be content regardless of circumstances

How much do you think Paul would have learned had he complained and grumbled instead of choosing to rejoice?

What effect do you think grumbling and complaining would have had on his attitude and his ministry?

planted obstacle

24

How did Paul feel about the help the Philippians had just sent?

grateful thankful using it as a chance to teach

What did Paul say would be the result of their giving (see v. 17)?

"credit to their account"

How did Paul say that God viewed this offering (see v. 18)?

fragrant pleasing acceptable

What was Paul's promise to them (see v. 19)?

God will meet all their needs

In what way do you feel that the promise in verse 19 is related to the fact that the Philippians had first given themselves to the Lord?

If you have a wrong motive & catch yourself confess it —

In what way is the promise related to their generosity in sharing beyond their ability to give (see Matthew 6:33)?

Seek first His Kingdom & righteousness & all will be given to you

8. Read Philippians 2:14-16. What was Paul's command to the Philippians (see v. 14)?

Do everything w/out complaining or arguing — to be blameless & pure — shining like stars in the universe —

For what reasons (see vv. 15,16)?

What effect does grumbling or disputing have on our witness?

belies it -

What effect does rejoicing have?

amplifies, stimulates, invites

Complaining, grumbling and bickering can be compared to covering a head-light with mud. The light is still there but it is so covered with mud that it is useless. A grumbling, complaining Christian will turn people away from Jesus. In contrast, a rejoicing, cheerful Christian will draw people to Christ like a powerful magnet.

What does Proverbs 16:24 say about pleasant words?

honeycomb - sweet to soul & healing to bones

What does Proverbs 18:21 teach about the power of the tongue?

power of life & death - to a relationship, to a psyche, to a

9. Read Philippians 2:17,18. What circumstances did Paul refer to that could have made rejoicing difficult?

to be poured out like a sacrifice - literally his future martyrdom could be death -

What did he determine to do anyway?

rejoice

[handwritten top margin: After 65 → McD - EGG CARTONS / house - then here for lunch/sleep / then McD babysitting]

What did Paul urge the Philippians to do?

[handwritten: Be glad + rejoice with him / Have Dad bring Wm to me at Widget]

Paul knew that his life could be taken at any time. Even so, he determined to rejoice and he urged the Philippians to rejoice with him. At this point in Paul's life, circumstances were difficult, but because Paul trusted Jesus, he chose to rejoice. Sometimes when we really feel like complaining, we must choose to rejoice. When we determine to rejoice and praise God even in difficult circumstances, God will change feelings of frustration into feelings of victory.

10. Read Philippians 1:12-20. What benefits of his imprisonment did Paul give?

[handwritten: gospel has been advanced - / - palace guard / other brothers / were encouraged to speak out / + everyone else -]

What two motives did Paul give for people preaching Christ?

[handwritten: - envy + rivalry / - goodwill]

How did Paul feel about the fact that some were preaching from wrong motives?

[handwritten: Doesn't matter - Christ is preached]

Why do you think Paul was able to have the attitude he had about those who were preaching from impure motives?

[handwritten: Focusing on the result - pragmatic - / ask: who are you trying to glorify?]

What other reasons did he give for rejoicing (see vv. 18-20)?

27

What confidence did Paul have in the Philippians?

they were praying for him

What part do you think Paul's confidence in God and in the Philippians' prayers had in his being able to rejoice?

power of prayer —

What role do the prayers of others play in the life of a person going through trials? Share a personal example of this from your own life.

Encouraging — surprising that others remember me enough

What was Paul's chief desire in life (see v. 20)?

Christ will be exalted — in Paul's life or death

What is your chief desire in life?

Be Fully realize as He would have me —

Had Paul's desires been wrong, he could have easily fallen into despair. However, he trusted Jesus and his aim in life was to always honor and exalt Christ. Because exalting Jesus was his aim, he could rejoice and praise God right where he was. He knew that God was working in his life and that Jesus was being exalted. Again we see that Paul chose to rejoice. Verse 18 says, "I rejoice, yes, and I will rejoice."

11. Read Philippians 3:1 and 4:4. What did Paul encourage the Philippians to do in these two verses?

Rejoice in the Lord

always

How often did he want them to rejoice?

always   w/out ceasing

A Closer Look at My Own Heart

12. Are there areas in your life that you need to praise God for even though they hurt? List those areas right now. Prayerfully lay them before the Lord and determine to praise God for the way He is working even if you cannot see His work. You might even want to draw a praise note over the top of your list as a visual reminder to praise and rejoice.

13. The psalms are filled with praise and thanksgiving. Read Psalm 33:1-3. What did the psalmist say about praising and rejoicing?

it's fitting & upright —   shout for joy

Read Psalm 50:23. What does this verse teach about thanksgiving?

honors Him — & prepares, shows salvation of God

Read Psalms 66:1,8 and 81:1. What is commanded in these psalms?

shout

sing

bless   proclaim

What is the main theme of these verses from Psalms?

Psalm 33:3, speaks of singing a new song to the Lord. A new song. A song that only you can sing. You can create your own song by writing a psalm of praise and thanksgiving to God. Look over the list you made in question 12; you'll want to include some of these things in your song. Then meditate over the psalms and write. Singing your new song out loud to the Lord can be the gift from your heart to the heart of your heavenly Father.

Action Steps I Can Take Today

It is important that we learn to say "thank you" and to express our gratitude to God. It's also important that we do the same to people. When the Philippians read this letter, they were probably filled anew with joy and an even greater desire to help Paul and others in the future. When others bless our lives, we need to encourage them by expressing our gratitude. It will strengthen them and uplift us.

14. Ask God to show you if there is someone to whom you need to express love and gratitude today. It might be the person or persons who shared the gospel with you. Determine to act upon what God reveals to you. It could be a note. A phone call. Let your attitude be one of gratitude.

Three

OVERCOME WORRY

In a sense, this lesson is a continuation of Key 2. Paul's greatest desire for the Philippian believers was that they "rejoice in the Lord always" (Philippians 4:4). But we can't experience joy, nor can we fully rejoice, when our hearts are laden down with worries.

Why? Because worry has the power to destroy our peace, our contentment and our joy.

Is worry robbing you of experiencing all that God has for you? In this chapter you'll see how Paul's trust in the Lord enabled him to face an uncertain future without worrying. If you will follow his example, you, too, can learn the secret of overcoming worry.

A Closer Look at the Problem

WHO OR WHAT IS IN YOUR HEART?

Before you begin this week's study, ask God to show you specific areas where worry is robbing you of contentment. Draw an outline of a heart in your journal and divide it into sections. Label each section with a specific person or situation you're worried about right now. Ask Him to reveal to your mind and heart His ways of overcoming as you work through this lesson.

1. Probably Christians worry most about the people they love. We want them to be in a right relationship with God. Read Philippians 1:3-6. What was Paul's attitude as he prayed (see vv. 3,4)?

What reason did he give for his joy and gratitude (v. 6)?

He knows God will complete what He started

What do you think would have happened to Paul's joy if he had spent his time worrying about how the Lord was working in these people?

Paul loved these Philippians, and it would have been easy for him to worry about them. However, his confidence was not in the Philippians, but in God's great power to work in their lives. When our confidence is in people and their power to stay strong in the Lord, we have reason to worry. But when we put our confidence in God's power to work in their lives, His comforting presence will give us peace.

A Closer Look at God's Truth

2. Read Philippians 2:13. What does this verse say that God is doing?

work in you to will & act to His purpose

What are some ways that God works in you to will and to work for His good pleasure?

I helps us see our own sin

Reword verse 13, making it applicable to you personally. Reword it to apply to someone whom you worry about.

God energizes our desires & actions

God wants us and those we love to grow. We don't always recognize the hand of God in difficult situations, but we need to trust that God is working to make our lives pleasing to Him. He is also concerned about the ones we love and is working in their lives as well.

3. Read Philippians 1:19,20. What indications do you have from these two verses that Paul was not worried even though he was in prison with an uncertain future?

through their prayers & help by Spirit of Jesus

List several things that Paul expected to happen.

turn out for his deliverance

Why did he expect these results?

whether by life or death — to be exalted — expect & hope —

Paul expressed his expectations from God. What effect did that have on his outlook in life?

In these passages Paul expressed what he expected from God. This process of affirmation is important in overcoming worry or other harmful attitudes. When we find ourselves worrying, we need to find promises in God's Word, then if we are fulfilling the requirements, claim the promises aloud. As we claim God's promises, our faith grows and our fears shrink.

4. Read Philippians 3:3. What did Paul say he would not put his confidence in?

no confidence in 'the flesh

What was Paul trusting instead?

we are committed to worship [illegible] the Spirit of God - we glory in Jesus Christ

What dangers are there in putting confidence in the flesh?

The flesh is the old nature that cries out to us to do things in our own strength, in our own way. Paul realized that neither he nor anyone else could find peace with God through his own works. He knew he had to put his confidence in God for growth and salvation in his own life as well as in the lives of others.

5. Read Jeremiah 17:5-8. What does God say about the person who trusts in mankind and in his own strength?

cursed

When we trust self, what does that show about our relationship with God?

our heart has turned away

How is the person who trusts self or the flesh described in verse 6?

like a bush in the wastelands —

How does this verse relate to a person's spiritual life?

it can make us isolated — dried up —

How is the person who trusts in the Lord described?

roots by stream — quenched no fear

To what is such a person compared?

What phrases in verse 8 imply a time of problems or difficulties?

when heat comes, year of drought will come but provision will be made

What is promised during times of trial?

no fear — never fail to bear fruit

What is the condition of these promises?

trust in the Lord

This passage shows clearly that if we trust in ourselves or in other people, the end result will be a life that is unfruitful. When we put our trust in the Lord, a fruitful, productive life results. Even in times of difficulties, we will not have to be anxious or fearful. Any time we begin to fear or worry, we need to recognize those emotions as a signal that we are not trusting God. We have either begun to trust ourselves or have begun to doubt God's power or willingness to work in this situation.

6. Read Matthew 6:25-34. In verses 25 and 26, Jesus tells us not to worry about our lives, what we eat, drink or wear. What reasons did He give for not worrying?

birds - lilies cared for but we're worth

Reword verse 26 to make it Jesus' personal message to you.

What does worrying accomplish (see v. 27)?

nothing - can't add to your life at all - robs you of today -

Why did Jesus say we shouldn't worry about what we're going to wear?

He knows our needs - its irrelevant

What command did Jesus give (see v. 31)?

What did Jesus say causes worrying (see v. 30)? *contrast w/ (look Hebrews 11:1)*

"little faith" -

What reason did He give for not worrying (see v. 32)?

our Father knows what we need - even before we ask -

When Jesus referred to the Gentiles, He was referring to those who did not believe in God. They did not know a heavenly Father that they could trust to take care of them. We, however, have a Father who knows exactly what we need.

In verse 33 what command did Jesus give? What promise?

seek first His kingdom & righteousness & all things will be given

What did Jesus tell us not to worry about (see v. 34)?

tomorrow

What reason did He give?

What happens to today's contentment when we worry about tomorrow?

takes it away

Jesus encouraged His disciples to trust a loving, caring heavenly Father who even takes care of birds and grasses. He encouraged them to make God's kingdom and His righteousness their top priority. When Jesus spoke of God's kingdom, He was referring to that realm where God is King. When we seek God's kingdom and His righteousness, we are seeking to make God the King and Ruler of our lives. When that becomes our number one priority, God promises to take care of everything else. Paul had done that in his life (see Philippians 1:20,21). As a result, he had assurance that God would take care of him. He saw no reason to worry.

7. Read Philippians 2:17,18. What was Paul's attitude even though he realized his life might be taken from him?

rejoiced anyway even though he might be poured out as a drink offering

8. Read Philippians 1:21. Paul said: "For to me, to live is
_____Christ_____, and to die is _____gain_____."

Paul was able to face such difficult circumstances without worry because he felt that whether he lived or died, he came out a winner.

9. Read Philippians 4:19. What did Paul say that God would do?

supply all riches, meet all needs

Because Paul didn't worry about what tomorrow held, he could rejoice daily knowing His faithful God was in control. Worrying about what the future holds does absolutely no good; it simply robs us of today's joys. In this passage Paul expressed his joy for today even though tomorrow threatened to be difficult. He also encouraged the Philippians to rejoice with him regardless of the circumstances.

10. Read Philippians 1:27-30. What phrases in these verses indicate that the Philippians were also experiencing some difficult times?

they were being opposed — suffer — struggle

In these verses what did Paul say was his desire for them?

to conduct themselves worthy of the gospel

What attitude did Paul discourage?

don't be frightened

How did Paul encourage the Philippians to look at the opposition and the suffering?

they'll be saved — by God + others will be destroyed

38

In verse 29 Paul indicates that the Philippians had been given the privilege of suffering for Jesus. How would that attitude affect a person facing an uncertain future?

Can you think of any reasons why a person suffering for Christ would be blessed? *a common bond*

the healing, the unexpected benefits or results –

Usually a person will not suffer for Christ unless he/she has a close relationship with Him. The individual with this close relationship will experience far greater joys and blessings than those who are not totally committed to Christ. The person who has a close relationship with God will not have to worry about future suffering because he/she trusts God to sustain and strengthen him/her through it.

11. Read Philippians 4:6,7. What was Paul's command about worrying in verse 6?

Do not be anxious about anything

Instead of worry, what attitude should accompany the Philippians' prayers?

thanksgiving

Why do you think Paul encouraged the Philippians to pray with thanksgiving about things that could worry them?

a reminder of blessings

What part should thanksgiving have in your prayer life?

What will be the result?

How is God's peace described?

guard / garrison the mind

A Closer Look at My Own Heart

In this study on overcoming worry we have discovered that peace is the opposite of worry. We've also discovered the power of thanksgiving.

When we pray about problems with an attitude of thanksgiving, God somehow takes those problems and begins to work miracles. The first miracle is His peace. When we worry, we open a door for Satan to steal our joy. If we pray instead, God shuts that door and His peace will guard our hearts and minds in Christ Jesus (see Philippians 4:7). When we thank God for the results we do not see, then God gives us faith to claim His promises before they are a reality. Trusting God to work gives us peace in place of anxiety.

12. Read Isaiah 26:3,4. What are the conditions for finding *perfect* peace?

steadfast mind

What reason is given for trusting in God? *trust in the Lord*

Rock eternal forever

40

The *NKJV* says, "You [God] will keep him in perfect peace, whose mind is stayed on You" (v. 3). Worrying is an indication that we have shifted the focus of our minds onto our problem and away from God, the Problem Solver. If by an act of the will we determine to focus on God and His strength rather than on our problem, He will give us His peace.

You can begin to do that right now by taking out the heart diagram you made earlier (see p. 31). Look at it, then determine to give God the worries you listed there. Write "To God" at the top, "From (your name)" at the bottom. Write Isaiah 26:3,4 underneath it and then draw an outline of a rock around the entire heart.

How does it make you feel to know that you have—in the best way you know how—given your worries to your Father?

relieved

freedom

yarn ball example

Action Steps I Can Take Today

Even though God has called us to trust Him, there are times when we simply do not know how to make this a reality. We want to trust, but somehow, we can't. Mark 9:24 is the account of another person who had difficulty believing, crying out, "I do believe; help my unbelief."

God knows the struggle you are going through and He wants to help. Ask Him for greater faith to believe and to trust that He will take care of your problems. Then thank Him for what He is going to do in your life.

13. Read Mark 5:21-24,35,36. What did Jesus say to Jairus (v. 36)?

Do not be afraid – believe

What is He saying to you?

14. Jesus does not want fear to rob us of the joy and peace that He came to give. Write Isaiah 26:3,4 on a file card. On the back write the following prayer:

> Lord, I admit I don't know how to trust and I know that worrying is a sin. You have promised that if I confess sin, You will forgive and cleanse. Right now, I claim that promise of forgiveness and cleansing, and I ask You to fill me with Your faith. I ask You to help my unbelief and teach me to focus on You and Your power. Thank You in Jesus' name for the victory that is mine.

Review your card every day this week.

Peace be unto you.

- Four -

RENEW THE MIND

We live in a negative world. Newscasters update us on the bad things that are happening around us. The media portrays the good life: the perfect body build, the biggest house with the latest gadgets, a vacation in Hawaii. Our minds taunt us, "Why not me?" Even employees and employers can't seem to find anything good to say about each other—or even about themselves.

This constant barrage of negatives can rob us of peace and destroy our contentment. And that isn't all. We all have within us a propensity towards the dark side. Paul wrote, "For our struggle is not against flesh and blood, but against the rulers, against the powers, against the world forces of this darkness" (Ephesians 6:12).

Although we can't remove all the negatives from our lives, we can guard ourselves against allowing them to control us. This chapter shows us how.

A Closer Look at the Problem

CHANGING OUR THOUGHT PATTERNS

Part of the reason Paul was content in all circumstances is that he had allowed God to transform his mind. This enabled him to experience peace and contentment. As we learn to change our thought patterns from dwelling on negative circumstances to focusing on the blessing of God, we too will experience the peace and contentment Paul knew so well.

Paul realized that the way a person thinks affects the way he or she feels and acts. A person who concentrates on the blessings of God will rejoice and experience God's peace. If, instead, a person dwells on everything that goes wrong, he or she will be filled with anger, bitterness, fear, hate and a multitude of other negative emotions. No one can experience those emotions and be content. Paul desired that the Philippians share the contentment and joy he knew, so he encouraged them to focus on positive things.

1. Read Philippians 4:6-9. List the things that Paul encouraged the Philippians to think about.

   What effect would thinking about these things have on a person's worry?

   Anger?

   Resentment?

   Hatred?

Do you think letting your mind dwell on these good things will help to bring peace and contentment? Why or why not?

A Closer Look at God's Truth

2. Focusing on Jesus renews our minds and gives us His perspectives on how to deal with negatives; only then can we have true contentment. Read Philippians 1:12-18. According to verses 12-14, what did Paul choose to let his mind dwell on?

Spreading the Gospel - all else's inconsequential

What adversities could Paul have thought about instead?

no privacy   no freedom   distance from friends

What do you think happened in Paul's life as a result of his choice of focus?

In verses 15-18, what positive fact did Paul choose to think about?

that the gospel was being preached

What negative condition could Paul have thought about instead?

wrong motives of others

What emotions could Paul have experienced if he had focused on the negative condition?

What emotions did he experience as a result of thinking about the positive?

Many people are robbed of joy when they allow their minds to dwell on some painful thing that another person has said or done. Whether the hurt was intentional or accidental does not seem to matter much.

In verses 15 through 18, we see that Paul felt there were people who were preaching to make him jealous. Had those negative feelings been his point of focus, he could not have rejoiced at the spread of the gospel. He probably would have become angry and resentful and His joy in the Lord would have disappeared. Instead, he chose to focus on the fact that the gospel was being preached and people were coming to know Jesus as their personal Savior. With his mind dwelling on that fact, he could rejoice and be content.

3. Read Ephesians 4:26,27. What do these verses teach us about anger?

   needs to be dealt / right away - don't stew + give devil an opening!

Relate Ephesians 4:26 to refusing to dwell on what makes you angry.

By setting a time limit (such as sunset), Paul insured that anger would be dealt with—gotten rid of—daily so that none of it could carry over even to the next day.

What are some hurtful situations that you sometimes choose to let your mind dwell upon?

family hurts

46

How do these affect your relationships within the home?

[handwritten margin note: Go to the throne before you go on your own or to the phone.]

The church?

At your work?

In Hebrews 12:14,15, we are encouraged to pursue peace, not anger. The implication in these verses is that an unforgiving spirit results in bitterness. How does forgiveness or lack of forgiveness affect peace and contentment?

How can bitterness make many defiled?

4. Jesus had much to say about forgiveness. Read the following verses and answer the questions:

Matthew 5:44—How did Jesus say we should treat those who mistreat us?

[handwritten: go + be reconciled   pray + love   because He forgave us - + meekness is not victimhood but is strength under control]

Matthew 6:14,15—Why is forgiveness so important in the life of the Christian?

Jesus asked us to pray for those who hurt or misuse us. When we obey His command, even though we don't feel like it, God will give us His grace to love and forgive that person. However, we need to realize that even though we

47

choose to forgive and pray for that one, the emotions of love may not immediately follow. Often the healing of wounds takes time.

5. Read Philippians 1:19-26. What did Paul choose to make the focus of his thoughts according to verse 19?

deliverance through their prayers & the Spirit

What positive aspects of death did Paul choose to think about?

to die was gain

What positive aspects of living did Paul choose to focus on?

What effect do you think his focus had on his attitude as he sat in prison not knowing what the future held?

In facing an uncertain future, Paul did not focus on all that could go wrong. He focused on Jesus Christ and the eternal reward that would be his. Often, when we look at the future, we tend to magnify everything that can go wrong. That becomes our focus and instead of peace, we experience fear and frustration. In order to find peace and contentment, we need to learn to focus on Jesus Christ and the good He can bring into the future rather than on the bad things that might happen.

6. Read Philippians 2:5 from several translations. What did Paul desire for the Philippians?

keep having attitude should be the same as Christ who didn't demand humbled himself not from selfishness but emptied

What effect would this have on their minds?

Their doubts?

Their forgiveness?

Their fears?

Their angers?

Their frustrations?

Their attitudes in general?

Since Paul's desire was that the Philippians have the same mind and the same attitudes that Christ had, we can know that it is God's will for us to have them too. However, this isn't always easy.

7.   Read 2 Corinthians 10:3-5. What kind of battle is described in these verses?

What kind of weapons must be used?

What did Paul expect to happen as a result of this warfare?

What kind of strongholds or fortresses do you think Paul was talking about in verse 4?

How are they destroyed?

What must be done with every thought?

There is often a battle going on in our minds that requires the kind of warfare that Paul described in these verses. Satan desires to build fortresses of anger, bitterness, pride, self-pity and a multitude of other negative emotions in our minds. He knows those emotions will keep the Christian spiritually ineffective and emotionally discontent.

For us to gain victory in Christ, we must bring these thoughts captive to the obedience of Jesus Christ. He has the power to change those thoughts if we are willing to let Him. When we experience a negative thought, we must bring that thought to Him and ask Him to overcome it. As we ask Him to replace our negative thoughts with His attitudes, we will gain victory over them.

8. Read Ephesians 6:11-18. Why is it necessary to prepare our minds with God's truth?

With what are we to clothe ourselves?

How do these verses from Ephesians suggest we might do this?

Why is the mind so important in the Christian's battle against Satan?

How do you think a Christian clothes his or her mind with truth?

9. Read Romans 12:1-3. What did Paul urge the Romans to do?

What kind of sacrifice is acceptable to God?

What were they commanded not to do?

What were they to do instead?

How did Paul say they would be transformed?

What steps do you feel a Christian needs to take in order to renew his or her mind?

Rewrite verse 2 in your own words. Make it applicable to you personally.

10. Read Ephesians 4:17-24. How did Paul describe the unbeliever's mind in verses 17-19?

What is the result of the condition of the unbeliever's mind?

Where is the truth to be found?

What is necessary before we can put on the new self?

How is the new self described?

What do you think Paul meant by his description of the new self in verse 24?

How is a renewed mind related to the new self described in verse 24?

Reword this verse to make it easy for you to understand.

When a person accepts Christ as Savior, he or she experiences a new birth. Although that person now desires to serve the Lord, the old human nature is still within him or her (see Mark 7:21-23). This results in a fierce struggle between the two natures, the old and the new.

As we allow Christ to renew our minds, the spiritual nature grows stronger and we become more and more Christlike. However, if we're to become more like Jesus, we must experience a renewing of the mind. Often as Christians we have sinful actions in our lives. When we desperately try to change those actions and bring our lives into conformity with Christ, we often fail and give up in frustration. Romans 12:2 shows us that the way to be transformed is through the renewing of our minds. When God's thoughts become part of our thoughts, our attitudes and emotions will be right. When our thinking is in line with God's thinking, the actions in our lives will also be in harmony with God's will and His purpose for us.

A Closer Look at My Own Heart

11. There is a thought-provoking story in John 5:5-9. In it Jesus asked a man who was paralyzed for 38 years, if he wanted to be made well. Why do you think Jesus asked him that question?

Why would a person want to be sick?

Do you think the man's desire to be well was necessary for Jesus to heal him?

What did Jesus command him to do?

How did he respond?

Before Jesus could heal this man, the man had to desire wholeness. The same is true with your emotions. You must desire God's contentment, joy and peace, or you will focus on the wrong things. At first thought, you would probably say, "Of course, I want to be content," but then you choose to let your mind dwell on what makes you unhappy.

Jesus commanded this man to arise and walk. In the same way, Jesus commands us to set aside self-pity and despair and to walk in the hope of Jesus Christ. You have a choice. You must truthfully answer Jesus' question, "Do you want to be well?"

MEDITATE AND PERSONALIZE

The only way you can develop a Christlike mind is to put the thoughts of Christ into your mind. His thoughts are found in the Word of God. As you memorize verses, personalize them and speak them aloud, God's thoughts and attitudes will influence your thoughts and attitudes. Your life will be transformed. You will reflect the power and love of Jesus Christ.

12. Read Psalm 1:1-3 and Joshua 1:8. According to these verses what are you to do with God's Word?

What effect will meditating on God's Word have on your actions?

What is promised to you when you meditate upon God's Word?

Action Steps I Can Take Today

13. Is there an area of weakness in your life that you need to let God transform? Write it here.

14. Find a Scripture verse that promises victory for your weakness and then memorize and meditate upon that promise. Personalize it.
    For example:
    - If you have a struggle with controlling your mouth, personalize and repeat over and over Philippians 4:13: "I can control my mouth through Christ who strengthens me."
    - If you have a problem with fear, memorize and personalize 2 Timothy 1:7: "For God has not given me a spirit of timidity [fear (*KJV*)], but of power and love and discipline."
    - If you struggle with guilt, memorize and personalize 1 John 1:9: "Since I have confessed my sin, God is faithful and righteous to forgive and to cleanse me from all unrighteousness."

15. Is there someone with whom you can be accountable concerning this area? Someone with whom you can share your weakness and your verse? Ask that person if he or she will pray for you each day this week.

- *Five* -

APPROPRIATE CHRIST'S RIGHTEOUSNESS

———

Nancy was what many would describe as a fireball Christian. She led a women's Bible study in her community and helped spearhead an organization to help the homeless. Whenever her children's schoolteachers needed something, they called Nancy. It was the same at church. Nancy organized socials and served on committees. She also served on the worship team and substituted in the Sunday School Department.

But instead of feeling joy and contentment, Nancy felt used and angry. She almost wanted to drop out of everything. But if she wasn't there, how would anything get done? Besides, her friends were always telling her what a great job she was doing.

What is Nancy's problem?

A Closer Look at the Problem

OUR WORKS OR GOD'S GRACE?

According to the religious standards of his day, Paul had accomplished a great deal for God. However, we'll discover in this lesson that he knew he could never gain Christ's righteousness through any of his own works. Paul's example is a constant reminder that no matter how impressive our spiritual accomplishments may be, they are worthless if we think they gain us any right-eousness. It is only as we appropriate Christ's righteousness that we are made right in God's sight.

The verb "appropriate" may be a difficult word for many to grasp. In its simplest form, however, it means, "to take for one's own." Just as non-Christians must realize they are powerless to save themselves, Christians must also realize that in their own strength and abilities they cannot effectively serve God.

As long as we depend on what we can do in our own strength we cannot appropriate the power of the eternal God. We struggle in our weakness because we are trusting our works instead of God's grace. When we depend on God's grace, we have the same power available to us that raised Christ from the dead. But how do we do that?

This chapter will help you understand how choosing to appropriate Christ's righteousness leads to contentment.

1. What are some outward actions that people trust in to make them right with God?

What dangers are involved in trusting our good works?

What are some of the ways you have tried to gain God's favor—either before you were a Christian or after you trusted Christ?

A Closer Look at God's Truth

This study in Philippians 3:2-11 opens with a warning. False teachers had come into the church and were teaching that circumcision was necessary for a man to become a Christian. Circumcision had been given to Abraham as a sign that his descendants were a people set apart by God as His own. Down through the generations all Jewish males were circumcised as a symbol that they belonged to God (see Genesis 17:9-14). If a Gentile wished to join the Jewish faith, he was required to submit to circumcision. These Jewish teachers who had come into the Church were now teaching that in order to become a follower of Jesus, a man needed to be circumcised and follow all the Jewish laws.

2. Read 2 Peter 2:1 and then refer to Philippians 3:2. What terms did Paul use to describe anyone who would lead someone astray with false teachings?

How did he describe the true circumcision?

Jeremiah 9:25,26 gives us insight on what Paul meant by the term "the true circumcision." In these verses the Lord declared that He would punish all who were circumcised (ceremonially clean), and yet were uncircumcised (unclean in their hearts).

According to these verses, what does the Lord desire: outward acts of righteousness (good works) alone or outward acts of righteousness combined with right motives and right relationship with God?

3. Read Philippians 3:4-6. How did Paul describe his works in comparison to the works of others?

List all the advantages that Paul had in being right with God, according to Jewish law.

What was his condition according to the Jewish way of thinking?

4. Read Philippians 3:7-9. What terms did Paul use to describe the way he felt about his works in these verses?

The Greek word that is translated "rubbish" (see v. 8) was used to refer to what was thrown away as worthless. It included such filth as the waste of slaughtered animals, and this is the way Paul had begun to look at his works. While he was trusting in himself, those works were keeping him from trusting God. In that way, they were a hindrance to him. They were worse than nothing because they kept him from acknowledging a need for Jesus. Just as we must throw away our garbage, we must also throw out all reliance on our works as a way of becoming right with God.

What reason did Paul give in verse 7 for counting these things as "loss"?

What things must we be willing to treat as garbage or rubbish in order to gain Christ?

Why is this necessary?

What did Paul gain by counting all works as rubbish and accepting Christ (v. 9)?

Write a description of the kind of righteousness Paul had before he trusted Christ (see also Isaiah 64:6).

FROM DEATH TO LIFE

Jesus came to this earth and lived a perfect life. He had no sin. Then He willingly gave His life as the perfect sacrifice to pay the penalty for sin. He came to bridge the gap between a holy God and sinful man. Our sins have separated us from God, but by accepting Christ's righteousness we are brought into a right relationship with God.

Paul was ready to throw everything away in order to gain Christ and His righteousness. He was willing to throw away his dependence upon his works, his position, his family, his wealth. He gave them all up to gain eternal and abundant life through Jesus Christ. As a result, Jesus took Paul's sin and exchanged that sin for His righteousness. In God's eyes, Paul became the righteousness of Jesus. God did not see Paul as sinful; God looked at Paul and saw Jesus' righteousness instead.

What about you? When God looks at you what does He see?

5. Read Philippians 3:10,11. What are the results of accepting Christ's righteousness?

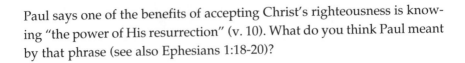

Paul says one of the benefits of accepting Christ's righteousness is knowing "the power of His resurrection" (v. 10). What do you think Paul meant by that phrase (see also Ephesians 1:18-20)?

Why is it necessary for us to consider our works as worthless in order to experience Christ's power?

6. In Philippians 3:10, Paul also speaks of knowing the "fellowship of His suffering." What do you think Paul is talking about?

In 2 Corinthians 12:7-10, Paul described a difficult condition he experienced. He called it a "thorn in the flesh." He said that God had allowed this even though he had asked Him three times to remove it.

How is Paul's reaction in verse 9 an example of Christ's power being glorified through Paul's weakness?

Why do you think God's power is perfected in weakness?

What part does realizing our weakness play in accepting God's grace?

How is this an example of the fellowship of suffering?

There are times in our Christian life when we go through periods of suffering and testing. Paul also went through these times. We need to realize that as we live the Christian life, there will be difficult times. However, God wants to use those times to strengthen us, and to bring greater spiritual growth and increased ministry into our lives (see James 1:2-4).

God's grace is the love and favor He freely gives us even though we have done nothing to deserve it. When Christians go through times of suffering, there are two ways we can react. We can reject God's grace and become bitter, or we can let God's grace comfort us and make us better. If we can recognize that even in this difficult situation, God is going to work for our good, then God's grace and love will comfort us and bring us peace. He can use our weakness and our suffering to draw us closer to His side and to bring glory to Himself.

When Paul spoke of the "fellowship of His sufferings," he recognized that when a Christian suffers for Christ, God pours out an abundance of His grace to comfort. If we will accept God's grace at that point, we will grow in the Lord and experience His peace and joy instead of bitterness and anger.

7. Reread Philippians 3:10. What does it mean for a person to become like Jesus in His death?

What is the result of being conformed to His death?

Paul's letter to the Roman Christians helps us understand what being conformed to His death means. Read Romans 6:1-14. In what ways are we to be conformed to His death?

What are the results of putting the old self to death?

In what ways does a Christian experience resurrection with Jesus?

What is necessary to experience that resurrection?

When Paul told of the benefits of having a righteousness based on faith in Christ rather than his own works, one of those benefits was that he might be conformed to Christ's death. Just as Christ had to put to death His own natural desires to live and to exalt Himself, so we must also put to death our natural desires to sin and be in control of self. But we need to remember that until we see our righteousness as worthless and accept Christ's righteousness, we can never put that old sinful nature to death. Unless we, through Christ's power, crucify the old sinful nature, we cannot experience the resurrection to new life in Christ.

8. Read Philippians 1:2. What was Paul's desire for the Philippians?

Who is the source of these blessings?

Which blessing comes first?

Why is it necessary to accept God's grace before we can experience God's peace?

A Closer Look at My Own Heart

Early in this study we looked at the life of a young woman named Nancy. Perhaps you saw a little bit of yourself in her—a driven woman, a tired woman, a woman so busy doing all she can do that she has lost her contentment and joy.

9.   What about you? In what ways can you identify with Nancy?

Compare Nancy's story to the word picture in John 15:4-8. In this word picture Jesus is the _____ and we are the _____.

What does He promise to do in verse 5?

Now ask yourself: *Have I ever seen a tree or vine work to bear fruit?* Of course you haven't. A branch bears fruit because it is connected to the vine. It is only from the vine that it receives power to produce fruit.

How would an understanding of this principle change Nancy's life?

How can it change yours?

PUTTING IT ALL TOGETHER

When a Christian tries to bear fruit in his/her own strength, he/she will begin to focus on his/her own works instead of on God's power. Then he/she will either become proud because of his or her own good works or become discouraged because of his/her failure. Either way, God cannot use that person the way He would like to.

If we will realize that our works will never make us right with God, we can get our eyes off what we can do in our strength and begin to rely on Jesus. He is the author and finisher of our faith. He is the only one who can bring us to our full potential.

Action Steps I Can Take Today

Read through the following questions. Choose one of the following that best describes the prayer you most need to pray right now:

❑ Is there an area of suffering in your life in which you need to accept God's grace and power to enable you to overcome bitterness and anger? Tell God about it, then open your heart to receive His grace.

❑ Is there some area of weakness that you need to praise God for because He can be exalted through it? Acknowledge that weakness. Thank Him for it. Ask for His strength and grace and believe that you will receive it.

❑ Are you trying to make yourself right with God through your works? Acknowledge that your works cannot make you right with God. Ask Him to forgive and cleanse you of all unrighteousness.

❑ Are you struggling to live the Christian life in your own strength? Praying the following prayer will help you acknowledge your weakness and open yourself up to His power:

> Lord, I acknowledge that I can never be right with You through my works. I acknowledge that I am weak and helpless in my strength. I accept Your strength and Your grace to empower me to live for You. I accept the righteousness of Christ for my own and I praise You, God, for exchanging my sin and weakness for Jesus' righteousness and power.

- *Six* -

*F*ORGET THE PAST

From Key 5, we understand that once Paul stopped trusting in his own works, he could forget the past with its failures and disappointments and move forward in a growing relationship with Jesus Christ. If we are to find true contentment, we must do the same thing. But how do we forget the past? How do we move forward with Jesus Christ? This chapter will help us discover how we can dismantle the roadblocks and begin to move forward in our Christian walk.

A Closer Look at the Problem

Consider the following scenarios:

> Mary slept with a lot of men before she became a Christian. Now she has met a Christian man who truly loves her and wants to marry her. But guilt over her previous relationships won't let her say yes to this young man. How can Mary be free of this guilt?

Paula, an older woman, has turned a lot of her friends away from God by harboring an intensely critical spirit. But instead of going to these people and asking for forgiveness, she makes excuses for herself: "Well, everybody has their faults."

Rene's husband Tom has a tendency to put things off. "I'll take care of that tomorrow," he says, but tomorrow comes and he doesn't do it. Instead of talking to her husband about how she feels, Rene lets resentment grow inside her. Resentment turns to anger, anger to bitterness. Rene wishes now that she had never married Tom.

Each of these women is facing a roadblock that is keeping her from growing in her relationship to Jesus Christ. All three of these roadblocks are rooted in the past. The goal of this lesson is to help us deal with the following critical issues:

- Guilt over past sins and failures;
- Refusal to go to a person we've hurt and seek forgiveness;
- Unresolved anger.

1. Think through the following questions:

What effect does my past have upon me?

What things in my past must I be willing to deal with and forget?

What happens if I continue to dwell upon the past?

A Closer Look at God's Truth

2. Read Philippians 3:7-17. What did Paul desire for his life?

What was his ultimate goal (v. 11)?

Did Paul feel that he had obtained perfection?

The Greek word translated "perfect" is a word meaning "complete or finished." Paul was saying that he was not a totally finished and complete Christian. In Christ, he had Jesus' righteousness, but as a human he still had areas that needed God's polishing.

What did Paul say he was doing because he had not yet obtained perfection (v. 12)?

For what reason?

Read verses 12-14 in several different translations. What do you think Paul meant when he said "in order that I may lay hold of that for which also I was laid hold of by Christ Jesus"?

How was Paul laid hold of by Jesus?

Paul was referring to a Grecian athletic race. The athletes raced with one goal in mind, to win the race. Instead of a string stretched across a finish line, as in modern races, there was a finishing post. The athlete who reached the post first grabbed hold of it, winning the prize. Likewise, Paul was pressing on to his finishing point. He wanted to lay hold of the prize—resurrection to a new, sinless, glorified body—which would live eternally with Jesus.

When Paul refers to being laid hold of by Christ, he is saying that Jesus reached down and took hold of him so that he could take hold of the resurrection available through Jesus.

3. What was Paul's objective (see vv. 13,14)?

What two things were necessary for him to achieve his objective?

Why do you think it was necessary for Paul to forget the past in order to "press on toward the goal for the prize of the upward call of God"?

According to Acts 26:9-11, what things did Paul need to forget?

How would Paul's ministry have been affected had he dwelt on those things?

THE PROBLEM OF UNRESOLVED GUILT

Guilt over past failures often keeps a Christian looking back. Unfortunately, when a person concentrates on past failures, he/she is more likely to repeat them. Fearing more failure and feeling he/she is not good enough to serve God, a person is hindered in his/her growth and ministry.

4. Read Psalm 32:3,4. List the results of guilt that you see in those verses.

These verses in Psalms show the devastating effect of guilt upon a Christian. Before a person can move ahead in Christ, sin must be dealt with.

Christians also need to realize that one of Satan's most effective weapons against them is guilt. He reminds us of our past failures and tries to deceive us into believing that God could not or would not forgive us for such a terrible sin. Just as Satan was overcome in Revelation 12:10,11 by the blood of the Lamb and the testimony of the saints, we can overcome Satan's attacks by using God's weapons. We need to claim the forgiveness that is ours because of Jesus' death (see 1 John 1:8-10).

ASKING FOR FORGIVENESS

Sometimes we find it difficult to leave the past behind because we haven't obeyed Christ's command to go to a person we have hurt and ask for forgiveness.

5. Read Matthew 5:23,24. What did Jesus command us to do?

Why do you think God commanded this?

How will it make a difference in our relationship with Him?

71

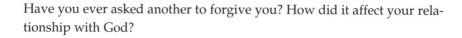

Have you ever asked another to forgive you? How did it affect your relationship with God?

With the other person?

How did you feel before and after?

In some cases, asking for forgiveness means making restitution. This is often very difficult to do, but the release of guilt and the love that God gives for that other person is tremendous. At times we have been only partly to blame for the situation, but we still need to ask forgiveness for that part, however small it may be. If we do not do this, every time we see that person or hear his/her name, we will remember the guilt and the hurt. We will not be able to forget the past and press forward in Christ.

6.   Read Psalm 32:1-7. What are the results of forgiveness?

DEALING WITH UNRESOLVED ANGER

Another area that often must be dealt with in order to forget the past is anger. Anger over something that has happened to us or to those we love can result in bitterness, hatred and unforgiveness. Many Christians feel it is a sin to be angry and deny their anger. This can have devastating results on our bodies and on our relationship with others. Anger in itself is not sin. Even Jesus was angry, but the way we deal with anger can be sin. If we stuff our anger inside and try to pretend it isn't there, we will be unable to forget the past and move ahead in Christ.

7.   Read Matthew 18:15-17 in several different translations. Who is the first person you should talk to if someone has sinned against you?

What will be the result if that person listens?

Why do you think Jesus commanded us to first go privately to the person who has sinned against us?

We need to be careful that while expressing our anger, we do not bring an uninvolved person into the picture and leave that individual carrying our wrath. When we tell others how someone has mistreated us, the person listening often becomes angry too. After we have worked through our anger, that other person may remain angry and unable to forgive. Jesus' plan is that we go directly to the person with whom we are angry. If we are afraid our anger may explode, we need to get alone with God and tell Him aloud all the hurts and anger we are feeling. Writing down the angry emotions we are experiencing before we go, will also allow a release of some of the tension.

Before we go to someone, we need to pray earnestly, asking God to give us His love for that person and asking for His direction as we go. We also need to ask God to reveal to us any areas in which we are to blame for the situation. If there are any, we need to ask that person's forgiveness before we express our feelings of anger. Then after expressing those feelings, we need to be ready to forgive.

8.   Read Matthew 18:21,22. What did Jesus teach about forgiveness?

What needs to be done after we have put the past behind us (see Philippians 3:13,14)?

Why is it important to reach forward?

What are some ways you feel this could be accomplished?

9. Read 1 Peter 2:2. What are we to desire?

What will be the result?

10. Read 2 Peter 1:5-11 in several translations. What qualities are Christians encouraged to cultivate?

What effort should be put into cultivating these qualities?

What results would we see?

What words in verse 8 indicate a growing relationship with God?

Why do you think it is important to have those qualities in increasing amounts?

In verse 10 what does Peter ask us to do?

What does God promise to one who is growing and practicing his/her Christianity? (vv. 10,11)?

A Closer Look at My Own Heart

In 2 Peter 1:5-11, you are encouraged to examine your life to make certain that you belong to God. What is God saying to you?

One characteristic of a true child of God is a desire to grow and become fruitful in God's kingdom. When we are in a growing and fruitful relationship with God, we will not be constantly stumbling. In contrast, the Christian who is not growing is usually going backwards and is open to numerous attacks from Satan. An immature Christian stumbles often and is probably one of the most discontented of God's creations.

11.   Read 2 Corinthians 4:16. What does Paul say about his inner self?

How do you think his inner self was being renewed?

Do you think it is important that it was being renewed daily? Why or why not?

12. Read Philippians 1:6. What is God seeking to do in your life?

How long will this process go on?

God's desire is to perfect (complete) each one of us. What are some ways in which you restrict God's work to perfect your life?

How does this affect your joy and contentment?

What do you need to do to allow God to do His work of perfecting in your life?

Paul would never have found contentment in Christ had he not been a growing Christian. The same is true today. The Christian who is not growing is not content. If our desire is to press forward in Christ to our highest potential, it is essential that we spend time with God and His Word. The Scriptures are our spiritual food, and without them we will be weak, ineffective and discontented Christians.

Just as we need the Scriptures, we also need the help and encouragement of other believers. We are not strong enough to fight Satan's attacks alone. We need the strength of God's Word and the support of God's people (see Hebrews 10:24,25).

Sometimes Christians feel they are strong enough in the Lord and don't need the support of other Christians. This is one of Satan's deceptions. God commands us to stimulate one another to love and good works and to encourage each other. We cannot do this if we are not getting together. We cannot help to carry their burdens, nor can they bear ours (see Galatians 6:2). We need other believers to help us grow in the Lord.

Action Steps I Can Take Today

13. Choose one of the following action steps that most closely matches your present spiritual need:

  a. If you have a problem with guilt because of past sins, read Romans 8:1 and Colossians 1:21,22. What do these verses say about those who are in Christ Jesus?

  How do these verses make you feel about yourself?

  Appropriate one of the verses for yourself by either memorizing or paraphrasing it in your own words.

b. Is there someone you need to ask to forgive you? If there is, go to God in prayer. Ask Him to give you wisdom, insight and courage. Also ask a Christian friend to pray with you and for you. Ask him or her to keep you accountable to do what you know God is calling you to do.

c. Is there anger in your life that you need to deal with? Reread the section on "Dealing with Unresolved Anger." Prayerfully consider how God wants you to deal with your specific anger. Then ask a Christian friend to be your prayer partner as you act upon what He reveals to you.

d. Do you want to grow in the Lord? If so, determine to make it a practice to meet with other believers regularly and spend time daily in God's Word. Ask God to give you a partner who will encourage you in these areas on a regular basis—someone you can also encourage in the same way.

Seven

OBEY GOD

—∞∞∞—

When God spoke to him, Paul immediately obeyed. One of the reasons he was able to do so was that he had his eyes on eternal benefits. He sought to lay up treasures in heaven rather than on earth.

As we study this chapter, we will see the importance of obeying God. We will also see how seeking an eternal reward rather than earthly possessions will help us find peace and contentment even in difficult circumstance.

A Closer Look at the Problem

It isn't always easy to obey God, but it is even harder on us when we choose not to obey Him. Disobedience always carries a price tag. The price is always high.

1. Read Philippians 4:9. What did Paul urge the Philippians to do?

What is promised to those who practice these things?

Share an experience in your life when disobedience kept you from peace with God.

Also share an experience in which obedience brought you peace with God.

Disobedience robs many Christians of peace and contentment. If there is some area of willful disobedience in our lives, we cannot experience total peace with God. When we knowingly continue to commit sin, it creates a barrier between us and God (and ultimately punishment if we don't repent). We hesitate to come into His presence because we know the sin is there and guilt robs us of our joy in the Lord.

One of the consequences of continuing disobedience is guilt that will not go away. Key 6 dealt with how to remove guilt due to past experiences, but if we continue to sin, we will continue to experience guilt. That guilt will keep us from finding joy and peace with God. We must repent of that sin in order to find peace. This means that we, through God's power within us, stop sinning.

It means that we develop a lifestyle of obedience to Jesus Christ.

A Closer Look at God's Truth

One of the most important things we can learn from the apostle Paul is obedience. His focus was on Jesus and because it was, he could exhort the Philippians to watch him and do the things he did.

2. Read Acts 16:9,10. What direction did Paul receive from God in these verses?

How long did it take him to obey?

3. Read Acts 26:16-19. What was Paul's response to God's vision?

What do these Scriptures from Acts tell you about Paul's relationship with God?

4. Read Philippians 3:12-18. What attitude did Paul encourage in those who want to mature in the Lord?

How would that attitude help a person towards perfection or maturity?

What did Paul encourage (see v. 16)?

What does verse 17 encourage?

What did Paul warn in verse 18?

How do verses 17 and 18 apply to us today?

What responsibilities do we have to those who may be watching us and following our example?

5. Read Philippians 2:12-16. What role does obedience play in working out our salvation?

What did Paul say the Philippians had done before?

What did he encourage them to continue?

When Paul spoke of "working out our salvation" (Philippians 2:12), he did not mean that we are saved by our own works. He meant that we our responsible for cooperating in the process of our own sanctification. Sanctification is the process by which we become more like Christ and in which our salvation is perfected. By our freewill, we unite ourselves to Christ, agree to be transformed by God's grace and experience His eternal presence. But ultimately it is God who works in us to make us holy, set apart for His purposes according to His will (see Philippians 2:13).

God has invited us to be saved and to be made holy. It is up to us to believe in Jesus and accept what He has done for us (see John 6:27-29). Once we have received Christ, we have a responsibility to work toward spiritual growth in Christ, accepting Him as master of our lives and allowing Him to take control. Unless we are willing to obey, we will not grow in Him and we will not experience His peace and contentment.

6. Read Philippians 2:13-16 in several different translations. What is God's part in our growth and obedience?

   According to verse 14, what should our attitude be as we obey?

   What are the results of cheerful obedience?

   What part does obedience play in proving ourselves "blameless and innocent"?

   How does our obedience affect other people?

7. Read 1 Peter 3:1,2. What result of obedience is found in these verses?

If we want to be able to reach other people for God, our obedience to Him is essential. We cannot be a light to the world and continue to live in sin. People see the way we act and our sinful actions negate our words. We will also be reluctant to share because we feel defeated and our peace and contentment have disappeared.

8. Read Philippians 1:27,28. What did Paul urge?

How would you describe a life that is lived in a manner worthy of the gospel of Christ?

What will be the results?

How does obedience help us to stand firm in the Lord?

How does obedience unite believers?

When Christ died on the cross, He conquered Satan and freed us from Satan's power. A believer does not have to be a slave to sin. We have a choice. Paul was asking the Philippians to choose to live a life of victory over sin rather than a life of surrender to sin.

9. Read Romans 6:1-18 in several different translations. List all verses that tell us we are not to continue to sin.

How should we live, according to verse 4?

How did Jesus make this possible?

How are we to think of ourselves (see v. 11)?

What happens when we believe God's power is greater than the power of sin?

List all verses which imply we have a choice of whether we serve Christ or sin.

What is the result of our choice?

List all verses that indicate we are not powerless to allow sin to control us.

One reason many Christians live defeated and unhappy lives is because we do not claim the power of God to overcome sin. We try to obey in our strength and we fail. We try again and we fail again. After awhile we quit trying because we feel it is useless to fight. God, however, has promised that no temptation is greater than we can overcome. He is faithful to provide a way of escape (see 1 Corinthians 10:13).

Our responsibility is to choose to ask for His help and to take the way of escape that He provides. If every time we face a temptation we would stop and ask God for His power that overcame sin at the cross, He will provide an escape for us. Sometimes, we, as Christians, do not want God's way in our lives and we do not ask for His help. As a result, we continue to fall victim to sin's power and are miserable, discontented people.

10.   Read John 15:10,11. What did Jesus promise to those who obey?

11.   Read James 1:22-27. How is the person who hears the Word, but does not act upon it described?

How is the person who hears God's Word and responds with obedience described?

What is pure religion?

We see from these verses that pure religion in the sight of God is a religion that produces action. We can study God's Word all day and be with God's people often, but unless we are willing to obey God, our religion is empty and we are deluding ourselves.

12. Read Philippians 3:17-21. What had caused Paul to weep?

How did Paul describe them?

What effect does our goal in life have upon our obedience to God?

How can Christians become enemies of the Cross?

What was Paul's focus in verses 20 and 21?

How did his focus affect his style of living (see v. 17)?

If we want to obey God, we need to seek what is eternal rather than striving for earthly rewards. The people that Paul described as enemies of the Cross had sought earthly rewards and as a result their lives failed to honor God and had actually damaged the cause of Christ. In contrast, Paul's focus on an eternal goal lead to an exemplary life that others could follow.

13.   Read Colossians 3:1,2. What did Paul urge the Colossians to seek?

What was Paul's focus of attention in the following verses?

Romans 8:18

2 Corinthians 4:16—5:10

Philippians 1:21-23

Philippians 3:11

Philippians 3:14

How did Paul's focus and goal help him to obey?

What effect did they have on his joy and contentment?

Think back to the last time you willingly chose to disobey God. What was your focus at that time?

What happened to your joy and contentment?

Many people are putting all their energies into seeking and caring for earthly treasures. We work so hard for material possessions and we neglect to lay up treasures in heaven. We don't have the time or energy to work on a right relationship with God or get involved with helping others to know the Lord. We don't have the time and energy to train our children in the Lord or to teach them to pray. We don't have enough money left to give to the Lord; we're too busy paying for and caring for our material possessions. Yet material possessions can never bring lasting joy or contentment (see Matthew 16:26).

A Closer Look at My Own Heart

One reason Paul found contentment was because he was seeking heavenly treasures. Things of this earth were not important to him. Being in prison could not take away from his goal. Being hungry did not change his focus. In the same way, if we desire God's contentment, we must get our focus and our desire off earthly things and onto spiritual goals.

Jesus emphasized the difference between the earthly and the spiritual when He instructed His followers to lay up "treasures in heaven" rather than "treasures on earth."

14. Read Matthew 6:19-21. How can you lay up treasures in heaven?

What part does obedience play in laying up treasures in heaven?

How do you think laying up treasures in heaven will affect your joy and contentment?

Action Steps I Can Take Today

15. Write down a spiritual goal that you would like to make your focus this year. Share your goal with a Christian friend. You might even want to get together and brainstorm practical ideas/ways that will help you attain your goal.

16. Philippians 4:13 states that you can do all things through Christ who strengthens you. Rewrite this verse to claim victory over a sin you want to overcome. Every time you are tempted, claim that victory and ask God for His power to overcome. He will not fail you.

- Eight -

Set Proper Priorities

In the last chapter we learned the importance of keeping our focus on Jesus Christ. We also learned the importance of making spiritual goals. In this chapter we will learn more about setting priorities that please God and result in the joy that comes from giving and receiving love.

Because Paul was seeking eternal goals, he had the right priorities in life. In order for us to have contentment in Christ, we also need to get our priorities straight. As we make pleasing God our number one priority, we will reach out to others with the love and unselfishness of Christ.

A Closer Look at the Problem

HOLDING ON TO OUR RIGHTS

This lesson shows us that an important characteristic in Paul's life that led to his contentment was his following Jesus' example of humility and unselfishness. Paul did not seek to advance his own cause. Instead, he willingly gave of himself so that others could benefit. Because he did, he was not susceptible to the depression that can come when personal desires are denied.

Often, we try to grasp what we think can make us happy. We try to hang on to our rights, our needs, our desires, and we end up being miserable. Jesus willingly gave up His position of equality with God to meet our needs. As a result, God has exalted His name above all names and given Him great honor.

When we give up our rights and our desires and put the needs of others first, we will find a joy and contentment that can never come from grasping our rights. When we put others first, God will exalt us and give us His peace and contentment.

A Closer Look at God's Truth

1. Read Philippians 1:20-22. What does Paul want to accomplish with his life?

   What do you think Paul meant when he said, "For to me to live is Christ"?

2. Read 2 Corinthians 5:9. What was Paul's goal?

   How do you think Paul's goal affected his relationship with other people?

   How do you think it affected his peace and contentment?

These verses demonstrate that Paul's goal was to honor Christ and be pleasing to Him. He wanted to live in such a way that he would never bring shame to Christ. Because honoring Christ was his goal, *circumstances* could not stop him from achieving it. Being in prison, being hungry or cold, other people and their opinions could not keep him from honoring Christ and pleasing Him. That rested in *his* control. In the same way, we choose where we set our priorities. If our top priority is to please God, no outside influence can keep us from our goal.

3.   Read Philippians 2:1-11. Compare Jesus' goal in life to Paul's goal. How are they similar?

What was necessary in Jesus' life for Him to accomplish His goal?

List all phrases that show who Jesus was and what He became for us (see vv. 5-8).

How does verse 4 relate to what Jesus became?

What did Jesus do when he became a man (see v. 7)?

What could Jesus have held on to instead (see v. 6)?

How do you think Jesus "emptied Himself" (v. 7, *NASB*) or "made himself nothing" (*NIV*)?

What indication do we have that Jesus had a choice in this matter?

Choosing humility and unselfishness goes against our human nature. We want to feel important and have all our needs met, but Jesus did just the opposite. He emptied Himself by giving up both his human and divine rights.

How did Paul define unselfishness (see v. 4)?

How did Paul define humility (see v. 3)?

What was the result of Jesus' unselfishness and humility for us?

What result was there for Him (see vv. 9-11)?

How does unselfishness affect our learning to be content?

What effect does humility have?

How would following Jesus' example of humility and unselfishness affect your life?

What changes would result?

What difference would it make in the lives of those around you?

Paul knew that Christians living together in harmony had power to impact the world. Therefore he encouraged the Philippians to be of one mind and one heart (see v. 2).

What would a united church show (see v. 1)?

How do Paul's instructions in verses 3 and 4 relate to a united church?

4. Read Philippians 4:1-5. Find phrases that show Paul's love for the Philippians.

What instruction did he give (see v. 1)?

What did he urge Euodia and Syntyche to do?

What did he urge the rest of the Philippians to do for Euodia and Syntyche?

What had these women done in the past?

What did he encourage everyone to do in verse 5?

How would the instructions in verse 5 help them to live in harmony?

The Body of Christ is in danger when even two members are not living in harmony. A divided church may begin with just two people disagreeing; before long, there is an ugly division. Paul urged these two women to have a gentle, forbearing spirit that would allow them to forgive and continue loving even after being hurt.

A divided church cannot move forward. Unbelievers, associating the bickering and lack of love they see with Christ, want no part of the church or its Savior. The lack of contentment will be obvious to believers, as well. Christians will find worship difficult because there is a tension that makes it hard to feel the presence of God. Contentment and joy disappear.

5. Read Philippians 1:7-11. How did Paul express his love for the Philippians in these verses?

What kind of affection did he feel for them?

What do you think is meant by the affection of Jesus Christ?

How is Christ's love different from natural love?

What was Paul's prayer for the Philippians?

Why does love need to have knowledge and discernment?

Is it possible to love someone in a way that is not beneficial for that person? Can you give an example?

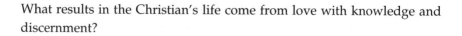

What results in the Christian's life come from love with knowledge and discernment?

How can love with knowledge and discernment help us "approve the things that are excellent" (v. 10)?

What will be the result for God?

Who is the source of this fruitfulness?

In these verses Paul expressed his love for the Philippians. As they had worked together and shared in his joys and sorrows, he had come to love them deeply. In the same way, when we share our hurts, our joys and our ministries, we will grow to deeply love those who become our partners.

Paul also expressed a need for them to have the right kind of love. Jesus' love showed itself in a servant's attitude and humility and that is what we need. But there are times when Christ's love also says no.

We need to be careful how we love. Sometimes our love can be grasping, smothering, overprotective or overpermissive. We need to pray for God's knowledge and discernment so that our love will be beneficial to us, to the person we love and to the kingdom of God.

6. Read John 15:9-13. What did Jesus promise (see v. 10)?

What was the condition of the promise?

Why did Jesus say these things to them (see v. 11)?

What commandment did he give in verse 12?

How does the commandment in verse 12 relate to the promises in verses 10 and 11?

What part does loving others play in our experiencing joy?

What example of great love did Jesus give (see v. 13)?

What proof do we have that Jesus loves us?

How does a person love as Jesus loved?

What difference would it make in the lives of those around us if we loved with Jesus' kind of love?

How do verses 12 and 13 relate to Paul's words in Philippians 2:3,4?

7. Read John 15:14-17. What are the results of obeying Jesus' commands?

What command did Jesus reemphasize in verse 17?

As Jesus taught His disciples to love one another, He gave them keys to open the doors of joy and contentment. (See John 15:11). One of the keys in verses 14 through 17 is the key of obedience.

The disciples could not experience the close relationship of a friend without being obedient. As Jesus gave them the condition of obedience, He also gave them the commandment of loving each other. As they obeyed, they would experience a special closeness to God and to fellow believers. They would produce a fruitful harvest and their prayers would be answered. Joy and contentment would result.

Jesus taught His disciples to love in the same way that He had loved them. This involves an unselfish love that puts the interests of others above the interests of self. One of our most basic needs in life is to be loved and to have others express their love for us. As we reach out with Christ's love, that need will be met. We will experience the joy that comes from being loved.

8. Read John 17:20-23. List all phrases from these verses that indicate Jesus' desire for his disciples to be united in love.

What would be the result for the world (see vv. 21,23)?

What part does the giving and accepting of love play in the perfecting of Christians?

Summarize in your own words why loving God and others is so important.

A Closer Look at My Own Heart

As Jesus pours out His heart in prayer to His Father, He again stresses the urgency of our loving one another. When Christians genuinely love each other, unbelievers notice the difference. If Christians loved as Christ intended, nothing could keep the world away. Genuine Christlike love makes the unbeliever want what the Christian has.

When Christians genuinely love each other, believers also benefit tremendously. We look out for each other. We help each other and, as a result, we encourage each other to the highest level of maturity possible.

9. Read Hebrews 10:24,25. What are we commanded to do?

What are some ways that other believers have stimulated your love toward others?

What can you do that will stimulate love in others? Be practical and specific.

10.   Read 1 Corinthians 13:4-7. How is love described in this familiar passage?

There are times when it may be humanly impossible for us to love a person who has hurt us or those we care about. During those times we need to be honest with God and tell Him exactly how we feel. Then we need to ask God to fill us with *His* love for that person.

It is important not to confuse feelings of love with actions of love described in 1 Corinthians 13:4-7 and 1 John 3:17,18. God commands us to act in love. As we obey His commands, the feelings of love will follow. As we stimulate others to love, God's love will grow within our own hearts.

Action Steps I Can Take Today

11.   Is there someone you have difficulty loving? Memorize 1 Corinthians 13:4-7 and ask God to give you this kind of love. Paraphrasing these truths into a prayer for that person will further transform your emotions and your actions. You will experience God's love in its fullness.

12.   Review the things Paul wanted to accomplish with his life by reading Philippians 1:20,21 in several different translations and writing in your own words what Paul was saying. How do his priorities compare with yours?

How will your tomorrows be different because of the priorities you're choosing today?

– Nine –

DEVELOP YOUR MINISTRY

In the last lesson, we saw that Paul's aim in life was to be pleasing to Christ. He wanted to honor and exalt Jesus in everything he did and because of this, his actions toward people were pleasing to God. He was able to reach out to others in humility with Christlike love. As he freely gave love, he received the joy of being loved in return.

One of the results of Paul's loving others was a desire to minister to them. As he served others, he experienced a sense of worth and accomplishment. In this lesson, we will see the importance of every Christian's having a ministry.

We will also look at some of the different types of ministry that are important to the Body of Christ today. Particular emphasis in this final chapter on finding contentment will be on the ministries of encouragement, giving, peacemaking and prayer. We will also look at how the discovery and development of spiritual gifts in our lives bring joy and satisfaction.

A Closer Look at the Problem

WILLING TO SERVE
Paul wanted to be with the Lord, but his love for the Philippians and his desire

to help them grow overpowered his longing. He knew that he was needed on earth and that his ministry would accomplish results. He was not afraid of work, nor did he expect others to serve him. His expectation and desire for life was fruitful labor.

Some people today look at the church as something to serve them and to meet their needs. However, one of our basic needs is to be needed and to be useful to others. This need can only be met as we are willing to serve others and become their ministers. Contrary to popular opinion, leisure time does not bring joy and contentment. Fruitful labor does.

A Closer Look at God's Truth

1. Read Philippians 1:12-18. What evidence of Paul's ministry, even in prison, do we see?

   What motives for ministry did Paul list?

   Which motives are noble ones?

   What was Paul's reaction to the wrongly motivated ministry?

   Why do you think Paul was able to rejoice even though some were ministering from wrong motives?

2. Read Romans 1:15-17. What was Paul's desire?

Why did he desire to minister in this way?

What do verses 16 and 17 indicate about the power of the gospel?

How do these verses in Romans relate to Paul's ability to rejoice even though people were preaching from wrong motives?

What do they reveal about Paul's ministry and his feelings about that ministry?

We can see from these verses that Paul had a ministry of preaching the gospel of Jesus Christ. He could rejoice when others preached, even from wrong motives, because he knew the gospel's tremendous power. The gospel changed lives and Paul knew that as people heard it, they would be drawn to the Lord in a faith relationship.

THE MINISTRY OF ENCOURAGEMENT
3. Read Philippians 1:21-26. What two desires did Paul express?

What reasons did he give for wanting to remain alive?

What do these verses reveal about Paul's love and unselfishness?

Why are these virtues important if we want to minister to others?

4. Read Philippians 2:19-24. How did Paul describe Timothy?

How did Timothy differ from the others Paul mentioned?

How had Timothy proved his worth?

What phrase shows Timothy's humility?

Why is it important that people minister with the right motives?

Why are proper motives important in finding contentment and peace?

Most Christians desire a ministry. We want to be useful, but often our motives are not pure. We want the jobs that will bring recognition and honor and tend to shy away from those that bring no glory. We would rather be an officer than be on the clean-up committee or nursery duty. In contrast, Timothy served with Paul like a humble child serving his father. He was willing to take the lowly position of a servant and because he was, God was able to use him and gave him an effective ministry.

5.   Read Philippians 2:25-30. How is Epaphroditus described?

What words show Epaphroditus's love for the Philippians?

What emotion did Paul expect the Philippians to experience at Epaphroditus's return to them?

How did Paul instruct them to receive Epaphroditus and why?

How did Paul look upon Epaphroditus's healing? Why?

Why do you think Paul felt the way he did about Epaphroditus's near death?

Why did he feel different about his own?

Paul had a deep love for Epaphroditus. In spite of his strong belief in a better hereafter with Jesus, Paul knew he would miss Epaphroditus if he died. We need to acknowledge that Christians go through difficult times and that it is normal to feel sad when we have experienced a loss or a deep hurt. However, God can and will give peace in the midst of those trials and will use them to strengthen us and enlarge our ministry.

Paul also instructs the Philippians to hold men like Epaphroditus in high regard. Honor and respect given to those who do the work of Christ can be a ministry for us and will encourage and strengthen those who serve the Lord.

6. Read Philippians 4:10-19. In what way had the Philippians ministered to Paul?

In what way was Paul ministering to them?

What was the result of the Philippians' ministry in Paul's life?

How did he describe their gift?

How do you think their ministry to Paul made the Philippians feel?

How does verse 19 relate to joy and contentment?

Do you think this promise is related to their willing ministry?

THE MINISTRY OF GIVING

7. Read 2 Corinthians 9:6-15. What does verse 6 tell us about our giving?

What are some other things that God may want us to give cheerfully?

What does God promise in verse 8?

List the promises found in verses 10 and 11 and give a spiritual application to each of them.

Promise   **Application**

How do you feel these promises are related to the cheerful giving of ourselves?

8. Reread verses 6-15. Giving liberally and cheerfully of ourselves results in an abundance for God, an abundance for the giver and an abundance for others. What gift do you have that God wants you to cheerfully share with others?

The promises of these verses are an example of the way God will bless us when we cheerfully give of ourselves to His kingdom and to the service of others. These promises apply any time we willingly give of ourselves and our resources in ministry to Christ.

THE MINISTRY OF PEACEMAKER

9. Read Philippians 4:2,3. What ministry did Paul urge?

What did Paul say these women had done in the past?

What term did he use to describe those who had ministered with him?

What did he say about those who had worked with him?

In these verses, Paul advocated a ministry that perhaps few think of as a ministry. He urged the Philippians to be peacemakers. Jesus came to make peace with God and with others possible. In the same way, God wants us to work toward bringing others to peace with Him and with one another.

He even promised a special blessing to peacemakers (see Matthew 5:9).

10. Read 2 Corinthians 5:18-21. What ministry did Paul have according to these verses?

What ministry of Jesus is found in these verses?

What results for you are found in this description of Jesus' ministry?

There are people all around us who need help in finding peace with God and peace with others. This ministry needs to be encouraged in every child of God. You can be part of it by asking God to bring to your awareness people whom you can help with a ministry of reconciliation. This involves a willingness to become involved with them.

THE MINISTRY OF PRAYER

11. Read Ephesians 6:18-20. Who did Paul encourage them to minister to in prayer? How often did he want them to practice this ministry?

Prayer is probably one of the most important of all ministries. We see that Jesus often arose while it was still dark to go and pray. Before He chose the twelve apostles, He spent the entire night in prayer. At Gethsemane He spent hours in prayer, gaining strength to face the cross.

Likewise, any effective ministry we are going to have must begin with prayer. Often, praying for people is more effective than preaching to them. There are some ministries that are open to only a few. Prayer is open to all.

SPIRITUAL GIFTS

12. Understanding our spiritual giftedness will also help us develop our ministries. Read 1 Corinthians 12. What did Paul tell the Corinthians about spiritual gifts in verses 4 through 7?

List the gifts and the ministries that Paul refers to in verses 8-11,28.

How does the example of the body illustrate the truths Paul was teaching about spiritual gifts?

How do verses 11-27 relate to the different gifts and ministries described in this chapter?

What truth do you think Paul was illustrating in verses 22-24?

What will be the result of accepting this truth?

What point was Paul making in verses 29 and 30?

Paul was stressing that not all Christians are going to have the same gifts or the same ministries. God created us differently and has given to each of us special gifts for different ministries. We should never feel we are more spiritual than the person whose gift is different from ours.

God planned us to be different and to work together as a body. People who we may feel are insignificant are tremendously important in God's plan. Sometimes a person's gifts and ministries are unseen by others, but they are seen by God and are essential for the functioning of His Body.

A Closer Look at My Own Heart

13. Read 2 Timothy 3:14-17. What will help prepare you for ministry?

According to these verses, what will the Scriptures do for you?

What part will the study of Scripture have in your becoming a more effective minister for Jesus Christ?

Often Christians want an immediate and glamorous ministry. We get frustrated at the church for not realizing our potential and providing us our desired place of ministry. We need to realize that we must develop a personal relationship with Jesus before He can give us a ministry. Sometimes He even has a better ministry for us than the one we think we want. If we take the time to develop our relationship with Christ, a ministry will naturally follow. This ministry will be a productive one for the Body of Christ and a source of satisfaction for us.

14. Look back over this lesson, then complete the following sentences:

Paul's purpose in life was...

Timothy's purpose in life was...

Epaphroditus's purpose in life was...

Jesus' purpose (see Matthew 20:25-28) in life was...

My purpose in life is...

15. Questions to ponder:
    - Will you seek to develop your relationship with God so that you can have an effective ministry?
    - What steps will you take to develop this relationship?

- Will you spend time with Him in prayer and Bible study?
- Are you willing to give of yourself to cheerfully minister to others?
- Are you willing to carefully examine the spiritual gifts and see what gift you have that you can share with others?

The way you answer these questions will make a difference today, and in eternity.

———◦/◦/◦———

A Prayer

Lord,

I want to be used by You. I ask that You develop within me a close relationship to You that will overflow to bless the lives of others. Give me the desire and the willingness to spend the time necessary to develop that relationship. Establish within me a servant's heart that will give cheerfully of myself and my resources to You and to others. Thank You for the ministry You are developing in me right now.

———◦/◦/◦———

Action Steps I Can Take Today

As you complete this Bible study, remember this: Jesus Christ came that you might have life abundantly. His desire for you is that you experience peace, joy and contentment, not just now in the present but throughout eternity.

Post the following verse where you can see it. As you walk through your day, rejoice. As you serve Him, sing. He loves you and will work all things together for your good.

For to me, to live is Christ, and to die is gain. Philippians 1:21

What Is Aglow International?

━━∽◗◖◗◖◗∼━━

From one nation to 135 worldwide...
From one fellowship to over 3,300...
From 100 women to more than 2 million...

Aglow International has experienced phenomenal growth since
its inception 30 years ago. In 1967, four women from the state
of Washington prayed for a way to reach out to other Christian
women in simple fellowship, free from denominational boundaries.

━∼∿∿∼━

The first meeting held in Seattle, Washington, USA, drew more
than 100 women to a local hotel. From that modest beginning,
Aglow International has become one of the largest intercultural,
interdenominational women's organizations in the world.

━∼∿∿∼━

Each month, Aglow touches the lives of an estimated two million women on six continents through local fellowship meet-
ings, Bible studies, support groups, retreats, conferences and var-
ious outreaches. From the inner city to the upper echelons, from
the woman next door to the corporate executive, Aglow seeks to
minister to the felt needs of women around the world.

━∼∿∿∼━

Christian women find Aglow a "safe place" to grow spiritually
and begin to discover and use the gifts, talents and abilities God
has given them. Aglow offers excellent leadership training and
varied opportunities to develop those leadership skills.

━∼∿∿∼━

Undergirding the evangelistic thrust of the ministry is an emphasis on prayer, which has led to an active prayer network linking
six continents. The vast prayer power available through Aglow
women around the world is being used by God to influence
countless lives in families, communities, cities and nations.

Aglow's Mission Statement

Our mission is to lead women to Jesus Christ and
provide opportunity for Christian women to grow in
their faith and minister to others.

———∾∾∾———

Aglow's Continuing Focus...

- To reconcile woman to her womanhood as God
  designed. To strengthen and empower her to fulfill the
  unfolding plan of God as He brings restoration to the
  male/female relationship, which is the foundation of
  the home, the church and the community.
- To love women of all cultures with a special focus on
  Muslim women.
- To reach out to every strata of society, from inner
  cities to isolated outposts to our own neighborhoods,
  with very practical and tangible expressions of the
  love of Jesus.

———∾∾∾———

Gospel Light and Aglow International present an important
new series of Bible studies for use in small groups.
The first two studies in the Aglow Bible Study Series,
Shame: Thief of Intimacy and **Keys to Contentment**, will be
available through Gospel Light in the spring of 1998. Look for
others released in 1998 in the Aglow Bible Study Series on choosing to change, building better relationships and
God's character and the **Fashioned for Intimacy Study Guide**,
companion to the book **Fashioned for Intimacy**. For information
about these and other outstanding Bible study resources
from Aglow, call us at 1-800-793-8126.

Aglow Ministers In...

Albania, Angola, Anguilla, Antigua, Argentina, Aruba, Australia, Austria, Bahamas, Barbados, Belgium, Belize, Benin, Bermuda, Bolivia, Botswana, Brazil, British Virgin Islands, Bulgaria, Burkina Faso, Cameroon, Canada, Cayman Islands, Chile, China, Colombia, Congo (Rep. of), Congo (Dem. Rep. of), Costa Rica, Côte d'Ivoire, Cuba, Curaçao, Czech Republic, Denmark, Djibouti, Dominica, Dominican Republic, Ecuador, Egypt, El Salvador, England, Equatorial Guinea, Estonia, Ethiopia, Faroe Islands, Fiji, Finland, France, Gabon, the Gambia, Germany, Ghana, Greece, Grenada, Guam, Guatemala, Guinea, Guyana, Haiti, Honduras, Hungary, Iceland, India, Indonesia, Ireland, Israel, Jamaica, Japan, Kazakstan, Kenya, Korea, Kyrgyzstan, Latvia, Malawi, Malaysia, Mali, Mauritius, Mexico, Fed. States of Micronesia, Mongolia, Mozambique, Myanmar, Nepal, Netherlands, Papua New Guinea, New Zealand, Nicaragua, Niger, Nigeria, Norway, Oman, Pakistan, Panama, Peru, Philippines, Portugal, Puerto Rico, Romania, Russia, Rwanda, Samoa (American), Samoa (Western), Scotland, Senegal, Sierra Leone, Singapore, South Africa, Spain, Sri Lanka, St. Kitts, St. Lucia, St. Maartan, St. Vincent, Sudan, Suriname, Sweden, Switzerland, Tajikistan, Tanzania, Thailand, Togo, Tonga, Trinidad/ Tobago, Turks & Caicos Islands, Uganda, Ukraine, United States, U.S. Virgin Islands, Uruguay, Uzbekistan, Venezuela, Vietnam, Wales, Yugoslavia, Zambia, Zimbabwe.

*One extremely restricted 10/40 Window nation.

How do I find my nearest Aglow Fellowship? Call or write us at:

AGLOW
INTERNATIONAL

P.O. Box 1749, Edmonds, WA 98020-1749
Phone: (425) 775-7282 or 1-800-755-2456
Fax: (425) 778-9615   E-mail: aglow@aglow.org
Web site: http://www.aglow.org/

The Aglow
Bible Study Series

Shame:
Thief of Intimacy
Marie Powers

Powers exposes the characteristics, contributors, and the cure for this emotion that affects women, knowingly or unknowingly, throughout the world.

Paperback • $6.99
ISBN 08307.21290
Available April 1998

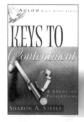

Keys to
Contentment
Sharon A. Steele

Journey through this study of Paul's life and teachings in his letter to the Philippians and learn how to find the contentment and abundant, joyous life that Jesus promised.

Paperback • $6.99
ISBN 08307.21304
Available April 1998

Building Better
Relationships
Bobbie Yagel

Use the Scriptures to build successful relationships with your loved ones, friends and neighbors, and learn how to handle confrontations and know when and how to seek forgiveness.

Paperback • $6.99
ISBN 08307.21320
Available July 1998

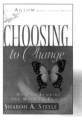

Choosing
to Change
Sharon A. Steele

Overcome rejection, guilt, fear, worry, discouragement and disobedience with the help of four essential steps to renew your mind and transform your life according to Christ.

Paperback • $6.99
ISBN 08307.21312
Available July 1998

Fashioned for Intimacy
Jane Hansen
with Marie Powers

Jane Hansen, international president of Aglow International, describes God's original design for men and women.

Hardcover • $17.99
ISBN 08307.20669
Available now

More titles in the *Aglow Bible Study Series* are coming soon: two in October 1998 and two in January 1999.

AGLOW.
INTERNATIONAL

Gospel Light

Ask for these resources at your local Christian Bookstore.